CANADIAN DISASTERS

René Schmidt

Scholastic Canada Ltd.,
123 Newkirk Road, Richmond Hill, Ontario, Canada

Acknowledgments

I would like to thank the following people for their invaluable help: James B. Brown, Marsha Drake, Professor Elliot Leyton, Carol Lindsay at the *Toronto Star*, Ken McPherson, Erik Schmidt, Anneke and Werner Schmidt.

For chapter two, "Canada's Worst Fire," Mrs. Esther Estella Dowson kindly gave permission to quote from *The Stonecutters of Old Toronto*, an unpublished manuscript by William Dowson in the Metropolitan Toronto Library's Rare Books Collection. In chapter five, the account by "Carla Sanderson" of life during the "Dirty Thirties" is an invention of mine, based on extensive research.

Canadian Cataloguing in Publication Data
Schmidt, René.
    Canadian disasters

ISBN 0-590-71525-9

1.Disasters - Canada - Juvenile literature.
I. Title.

FC176.S35 1986   j971.06   C85-098479-3
F1008.3.S35 1986

9 8 7 6 5   Printed in Canada   4 5 6 7 8/9
                    Manufactured by Webcom Limited

Contents

*I would like to dedicate this book
to eight young men I hope will continue reading
to the end of their days: David P. Allen,
Lorne R. Allen, Donovan Brown,
Shane Burnie, Jason L. Campbell, Stephen Ram,
John L. Sullivan, and Jason R. Wait.*

Introduction

Disasters can occur anywhere, and to anybody. You could be involved in a disaster today or tomorrow. Sometimes they are caused by human beings, at others by the powerful and deadly forces of nature.

Accidental explosions can kill dozens of innocent people in seconds. A jet aircraft crashes and hundreds die in a few moments of screaming panic. One earthquake can destroy a mountain, change the route of a river or flatten a city. Storms can create waves high enough to twist and sink ships that try to run against them. Fires can scorch thousands of hectares of bush or forest, or they can burn whole towns, leaving the inhabitants homeless.

This book describes some of the disasters that have happened in Canada over the years. They are all true events. Some could have been prevented. Others were unavoidable. Many produced heroes: ordinary people in ordinary places who saved lives by doing extraordinary things when calamity struck.

As you read about these Canadian disasters, think about what you would have done if you had been there . . .

1
The Bridge That Fell Twice

In the year 1900, a group of businessmen from
Quebec organized the construction of a bridge across
the St. Lawrence River near their city. They decided
that a particular American company had the
necessary expertise to build the bridge, but they were
wrong. The project was to become a major disaster in
which 75 workers were killed.

The company designed a long, elegant bridge,
the longest cantilever bridge in the world. A
cantilever bridge is one which is balanced so that
long sections can stretch out without being held up by
pillars. The design for this particular bridge,
however, was flawed. Theodore Cooper, the chief
engineer, knew this, but he chose to keep quiet. He
thought that the bridge, although weak, would still
be strong enough for the job. Cooper wanted the
assignment, and he was worried that if he pointed out
the flaws in the design he wouldn't get another

opportunity to be involved in the construction of something so magnificent. The chance for a proud end to a famous career would then be lost to him. He approved the plans and the construction of the bridge began.

John Splicer was a high-steel construction worker, one of the best. He was an Indian from the Caughnawaga reserve near Montreal. All the men of his band were famous for their fearlessness and skill while working in high places, and they should have felt at ease working on the new bridge.

But they were far from being at ease. In early August, 1907, John and his friends worried constantly about one of the bridge's "chords," the heavy vertical steel beams. There was a bend in it, and each day the bend grew noticeably worse. The foremen and engineers on the job tried to have the chord bolted and riveted back straight, but it didn't work and the bend only increased.

The engineers grew more and more alarmed. Finally, one of them went to New York to discuss the situation with Theodore Cooper. Cooper realized the weakness in the design was showing after all and ordered that work on the bridge be stopped immediately. But it was too late. On August 27, 1907, before the engineer could return to Quebec with the news, the bridge collapsed.

The elegant bridge was reduced to this in a few short seconds.

John Splicer wasn't on the bridge that day. He had been so nervous about going to work that he had stayed home in bed. But many of his lifelong friends had reported for duty as usual. Several were still on the bridge when, right around quitting time, chord A-9-L finally gave in to the stress and bent around like a pretzel. In less than a second, support wires and beams snapped loose and the whole structure fell. It dropped 50 metres before it came to rest in a twisted tangle of metal.

The centre section of the bridge, photographed as it was actually falling.

Half of the bridge fell into the muddy waters of the river, crushing or drowning those who were unable to spring away in time. Rescuers rushed in, but there was little they could do for the men trapped in the wreckage. There wasn't enough time to set up cutting torches before the waters of the St. Lawrence began to rise with the tide, and they could only watch helplessly as the men drowned one by one. Altogether, 75 workers died in the worst bridge-building disaster in the world, 35 of them from John Splicer's reserve.

But it didn't end there. Nine years later, in 1916, a stronger and better designed bridge was being completed. The last piece, the centre section, was being hoisted from barges floating on the river when, suddenly, a chunk of steel broke off and the whole section fell. Thirteen men perished.

Now everyone was nervous. There were those who claimed the bridge was cursed. Nevertheless, on September 20, 1917, apprehensive workmen finally lifted and bolted into place another centre section. The Quebec Bridge was finished at last, 89 lives and 17 years after it was begun.

Many have forgotten the story behind this bridge. But there are two groups of Canadians who will always remember it. The high-steel workers of the Caughnawaga Reserve near Montreal is one. After 35 of their number died in one day, the elders of the band made the men promise never again to work all together on one project.

The professional engineers of Canada is the other group. This disaster showed that even famous men can make tragic mistakes. When engineers graduate from McGill University in Montreal, part of the graduation ceremony is conducted in a room encircled by one of the large steel chains used in building the disastrous bridge. And it is said that the iron rings all Canadian engineers wear originally came from a girder taken from the Quebec Bridge. The rings originally were a reminder of what terrible losses can come from engineering mistakes.

2
Canada's Worst Fire

Fire these days, although dangerous and fearsome, isn't the problem it used to be. For early Canadians uncontrolled fire was always something to be dreaded. Firefighters in those days didn't have trucks and hydrants for water. If you lived in the country a fire in winter could mean death in two ways. You might escape your burning house alive, but freeze to death before you could reach your nearest neighbour. In the cities, a fire could demolish whole blocks of wooden houses before the flames burned themselves out.

But there is one type of fire where things have not changed. If a forest fire approaches today you do the same as you would have done 50 years ago. You run for your life to escape it.

Canada's worst fire was a forest fire that overran the entire town of Matheson, Ontario, in 1916.

William Dowson was only 19 when he lived

through the Matheson fire. His own words tell the story best. He was sitting in a small shack, talking with friends. They knew a forest fire was burning a few kilometres away from them:

"Whop! A terrific blast of fire-heated wind, accompanied by a thick pall of smoke, swept down from somewhere. The shack was shaken as though by a giant hand. We got out quickly, believing it was about to collapse, or catch fire . . .

"When I realized the terrible danger from this exceedingly unusual fire roaring down upon us, I hiked to my tent for road clothes. The great body of it was perhaps 10 miles away, yet I could feel the heat in my face, and on my back through my clothes . . .

"We began to get ready to leave . . .

"I had to get ahead of the main fire. If I were caught in this I would be cooked alive in a few seconds. In the distance it thundered; a continuous roaring sound like a freight train; ominous and deep sounding; such a powerful tone as is made only by a forest fire in dry time exploding into flame . . ."

A train came to pick people up. Soon after, the fire roared over the tracks, leaving them twisted and useless. William stayed in town:

"Then out we went on spark watch, and to try to figure out what to do to save ourselves and our settlers' effects. It was no use. There was no chance to stop the burning . . .

"For hours I had moved fast in temperatures that could have reached 130 degrees and much more . . . My legs let go. A voice reached me: 'Get up' . . .

"It was dark as night now, but still afternoon. This, my fatigue, the great dry heat, and the thick smoke made it difficult to breathe — although the smoke never was thick at ground level. The uprush of heated air carried it thousands of feet into the sky, and, I supposed, a lot of breathable air went with it. But more rushed in as wind under terrific pressure . . .

"Were we surrounded by fire? Was there any chance to escape somewhere? Then, a hundred yards ahead, fire . . .

"A wall of flame swept the opening. I hesitated. The comparative cool on the other side enticed me. I faced the fire and dashed through it, eyes closed, through a mass of red-orange flame. The great fire wrapped about me for a moment — a solid mass of combustion like the interior of a furnace. Then I was through and in a clearing . . ."

William Dowson collapsed in the clearing, but he was on ground high enough that he got oxygen, so he survived. Many others were not as lucky. Wading into creeks and rivers, they suffocated when the oxygen around them was used up by the fire. Others stayed too long to try to save their homes and were caught in the roaring flames. Later, William regained consciousness and explored the ravaged town:

"We lost all track of time. We just enjoyed the air, which seemed so clear and cool. All around us the great land glowed from the golden glow of the after-burning. Nothing remained but the fairly thick stubs of trees. Some of these burned like candles. In others, irregularly set pockets of fire glowed and sparkled. Occasionally a pocket near the base of one would burn almost through. Slowly it would bend towards the glowing earth, then, as its burning fibres gave way, fall quickly, to land with a soft thud, sending out from its sides clouds of soft ashes . . .

"There was no sound of trains. The railway was stopped. Out at Belleek Siding a larger fire burned a car of coal on the passing track. I remember its steel wheels slowly melting down to slump like mud around the steel rails of the track . . .

"I went to see if anything remained of Matheson. There was nothing north of the tracks, and that was nearly all of Matheson. Swept away, all of it. Only a few bewildered men-folks wandering about. And the word that the surrounding country was full of dead people. No one knew what to do, and the tracks south of the town were ruined, with perhaps bridges destroyed. Death and desolation under a bright clear sky and soft summer breeze. And it wasn't 24 hours since the black death had roared through . . ."

Two survivors of the Matheson fire stand amidst the burnt-out remains of their home.

The Matheson fire was Canada's worst killer fire. 200 people died in the heat and flames. William Dowson took the only photos of the destruction; otherwise the meaning of the disaster might have been lost. Dowson also told of the rebuilding of the town:

"The government built some small places for the elderly at their home sites. And they supplied lumber and building materials for replacements to full-size homes. But you had to supply your own labour. For the elderly this was an impossibility. There were no pensions, no welfare. There never had been. And there was little insurance coverage, even on places of business, in these small towns . . ."

The residents of Matheson rebuilt their town and it still exists near Timmins, Ontario, surrounded by hundreds of square kilometres of forest.

3
Death on the Ice

In Newfoundland, in 1914, the fishermen relied on the seal hunt for their livelihood. The two dollars they received for each pelt was the main source of their winter income. The men scrambled to secure places on the seal ships, even though the work was unpleasant and the conditions aboard the ships terrible. The hunters had to make their own hot food on the open deck and find a place to sleep wherever they could. Many of the ships' captains cared nothing for the sealers. All they were interested in was loading up with as many pelts as they could carry.

In 1914 an old wooden ship, the *Newfoundland*, set off with a full load of fishermen for the seal hunt, but the underpowered vessel got stuck in the ice. Captain Wes Keane knew that the *Stephano*, commanded by his father, was very close to the seals. After being stuck three days, he suggested to the men that they walk across the ice to the hunt. If the weather deteriorated they could take shelter on his father's ship.

After a long, cold walk, the men found no seals, but came upon old Captain Abram Keane and the *Stephano*. He took them aboard and sailed to the site of the hunt, where he dropped them off. Before leaving them, he told the sealers not to return to his vessel, but to walk back to their own ship after the hunt. Nobody dared question the powerful old captain, and when the time came, they set out on the long walk back to the *Newfoundland*.

About halfway back, a blinding storm swooped down on them and within moments all the landmarks looked the same. The *Newfoundland* had no radio aboard, so Wes Keane, not knowing that the men were supposed to be returning to his ship, believed the hunters to be safely aboard the *Stephano*. His father assumed they were back aboard the *Newfoundland*. Nobody had any idea that the men were missing, lost on the ice.

For two days the hunters suffered and died. One of them, Jessie Collins, bravely pushed, slapped and cheered the men on, keeping them moving — keeping them alive. But despite his untiring efforts, many men simply froze to death where they stood, or while praying, or when they fell asleep. A father was found standing with his sons, their arms around each other, frozen to the spot. One young man, Cecil Mouland,

The *Bonaventure, Florizel, Stephano* and *Newfoundland*. All these ships were involved in the seal hunt disaster.

kept himself alive by refusing to allow the idea that any other man should have the opportunity to marry his fiancé because of his death.

Finally, Captain Wes Keane spotted the frozen band on the ice, and the rescue was on. Out of the 123 who had set out, only 46 men were still alive. The blame was laid on the shoulders of Captain Abram Keane for failing to make sure the men were safe. As a result of this tragedy, all sealing ships were advised to carry radios and improve safety.

4
The Desjardins Canal Disaster

On March 12, 1857, a passenger train from Toronto was heading for Hamilton. Just before Dundas, a town on Burlington Bay, it started onto a short railway bridge over the Desjardins Canal. It never made it across.

On board were about 100 passengers, some of them important and influential citizens. There was Sam Zimmerman, a self-made millionaire who had helped build the Welland Canal, as well as the first suspension bridge over the Niagara River. He also owned hotels, real estate and two ships. There was Captain James Sutherland, a long-time sailor. He was famous as a naval officer, and then as a master on steamboats in Upper Canada. Both his brothers had died at sea, and now, in a way, he would too. And there was John C. Henderson, a brilliant inventor. Scientists all over the world knew of his work in astronomy and mathematics. Many other

The timbers of the wooden bridge gave way and one after another the rail cars plunged into the canal below.

well-known local citizens and businessmen were also on the train.

Just before 6:00 p.m., as the train headed slowly for the Desjardins Canal bridge, a switchman going off duty jumped aboard. Suddenly he heard the whistle sound, signalling that the brakes were being applied. He looked ahead just in time to see the heavy locomotive drop down through the floor of the bridge. The switchman leaped off the train and watched in horror as the coal car followed the engine. Next came the baggage car. Down it went. Then the first passenger car toppled into the canal with its full load of passengers. The second passenger carriage, the last car on the the train, teetered for a few seconds on the edge of the broken bridge before it too fell.

Passengers screamed and shouted for help. People ran from afar to come to their aid, but only a handful were rescued alive. About 60 people died in that train wreck, including Sam Zimmerman, Captain Sutherland and John Henderson. An investigation later showed that the locomotive had either broken an axle or derailed just before it came to the wooden bridge. The sturdy timbers couldn't withstand the smashing impact of the steel wheels and the train crashed right through the bridge.

If you look you will notice that most rail bridges now have steel sides. These sides are to keep the train on track and centred on the strongest part of the bridge if a wheel or axle breaks. We all learn from our mistakes, and railway engineers learned from the Desjardins Canal disaster.

5
The Dirty Thirties

Most disasters are quick and sudden. This disaster was just the opposite. Between the years 1929 and 1939, many banks and businesses all over the world collapsed. Millions of people, including thousands of Canadians, lost their life savings, their jobs and much of what they owned.

Hardest hit were the farmers of Saskatchewan and Alberta. At a time when people were so poor that they couldn't afford even a bus token or a sandwich in a restaurant, Saskatchewan and Alberta wheat farmers suffered the added burden of a long drought — a period when there is no rain and the land is baked dry by the sun. The "Dirty Thirties" were so named because the "dirt" of the prairies blew across the dry land in choking dust storms.

Carla Sanderson will never forget the Dirty Thirties. When she was 10 years old she had to share a pair of shoes with her sister in order to go to school:

"In those years — 1930-1939 — there was a terrible drought. No rain fell from one season to the next, hardly. Nothing would grow. We couldn't sell any wheat, so we got poorer and poorer. My sister Penny and I shared shoes. She would go to school one day, and I would go the next. It was a long walk and Mom wouldn't let us go barefoot. Some kids wrapped their feet in newspapers. Things just wore out. We had no money for new clothes.

"In later years the relief train came in and we got clothes and apples from people in the east. Lots of apples. Mom canned them and cooked them and baked them into everything. We got codfish from the ocean. Big, flat, dried codfish. We called them snowshoes. We had patches on everything. We wore patches on the patches.

"And the dust! Dust storms would come up and black everything out. They said you could reach into a dust storm and come out with a handful of dirt, and I believe it. It was all the topsoil blowing away. Maybe the Americans got it now. Who knows? But the prairies were like a desert.

"We lost our farm, Dad was so far in debt to the bank. He'd had to borrow just to keep us alive. Daddy let the farm go after '37. Seven years of dust and drought and it went on until 1939. The rain started, then, again, but it was too late for us.

A dust storm in Alberta during the Dirty Thirties.

"When we moved on, the schoolteacher, Dan Ferris, had to go too. He hadn't been paid in over a year. When Penny and I left, plus Rick, my brother, there weren't enough kids to keep the school open, so he had to go.

"Everyone from the city was trying to find work in the country. All us farmers went to look for work in the city. We stayed with Uncle Ray. He had a store. He nearly went broke because he let people buy on credit. In those days, that was like giving it away. Nobody could pay, it seemed.

This is how the countryside looked after a dust storm.

"Soup lines! People would line up for miles just for soup from charity. There wasn't any unemployment insurance in those days. People could have starved in the streets except for the Salvation Army and other charities.

"There was the Depression, see. Every big business seemed to be broke, not just in Canada, but the U.S. and Europe, too. People rode the freight trains to try to find work. Men went everywhere. Hobos, we called them until my dad joined them. After that they were men-out-of-work. He couldn't stand to see us living off Uncle Ray, and him just a mouth to feed. He rode the rails trying to find work. We hardly saw him for two years. He never was the same after. He had been so proud before. But after, well, the Depression never left him.

"None of us is the same since. I save everything. It's silly, but I can't stop it, can't stand to see food wasted. 'Give it to me. I'll put it in the fridge.' That kind of thing.

"The Depression ended. Well, I guess it was good that it ended. But World War II started. Hitler was a madman. Millions of people died because of him. But the war put everyone to work making airplanes, guns, you name it. The young men went to war. That's how the Depression ended. One disaster stopped and another one started. Kind of sad, isn't it?"

In 1939 the rain came again and the farmers were shown a new way to plow so that soil wouldn't blow away in dry times. The Dirty Thirties are unlikely ever to happen again.

6
The Dugald Train Wreck

It was the end of the summer holidays for many Winnipeggers who had been vacationing in the Lake of the Woods cottage country. They were travelling home on an old wooden passenger train which had started out from Minaki, Ontario, returning to jobs and schools in Winnipeg and nearby towns.

The train should have been taken out of service years earlier, but it had been kept running because of World War II. The war was over, but such trains had still not been retired, despite the fact that they were very dangerous. Made out of wood, they weren't nearly as strong as the new steel coaches. Besides, they were a fire hazard: instead of electricity, the cars were lit with gas, which was carried in large tanks beneath the coaches.

At 10:50 p.m. on September 1, 1947, the Minaki train approached a CNR transcontinental train stopped at Dugald, about 30 kilometres east of

Winnipeg. What the engineer didn't know was that both trains were on the same track. The Minaki train slammed into the transcontinental, and several of the old wooden cars derailed.

Gerald Shields was working just 100 metres away when the accident happened. He ran to the wreck and was able to pull five dazed passengers from the smashed cars before fire broke out and the searing flames drove him and other rescuers back.

Many people were still trapped inside the train, calling for help, but the fires were fed by broken gas lines and the big gas tanks themselves, and there was no hope for those who weren't immediately pulled free. Most of the more than 40 dead were in the first two passenger cars of the Minaki train. The transcontinental, a modern train with steel coaches, wasn't derailed by the crash, and its passengers were only shaken up.

The Dugald train wreck remains one of Canada's worst train disasters.

7

An Explosion as Big as a Nuclear Bomb

The worst disaster ever to happen in Canada occurred in 1917, in Halifax, Nova Scotia. Much of this busy sea port was blown up in the biggest accidental explosion in the history of the entire world. In a few terrible seconds, over 1600 people died and 6000 more were wounded.

It was World War I. German submarines were lurking underwater, waiting to torpedo English and Canadian vessels in the Atlantic Ocean. To guard against this, ships travelled in large groups called convoys, with navy warships to protect them. Halifax was where the ships came together to form the convoys.

On the morning of December 6, an ammunition ship called the *Mont Blanc* was entering Halifax harbour. A freighter, the *Imo*, was heading out. The *Mont Blanc*, as long as a football field and 20 metres wide, was fully loaded with high explosives. The ship

was, in effect, a huge floating bomb. For some reason, both ships steered for the same side of the narrow channel.

Big freighters are very hard to steer, and by the time the *Imo* began to change course it was too late. It ran into the *Mont Blanc*, ripping it open like a pop can. A fire started on board. The crew tried desperately for a few minutes to put it out. Then they dropped everything and ran, knowing the ship could blow up at any moment and kill them all.

Only a few people on shore knew that the crippled vessel they could see drifting in the harbour with blue flames licking from it was an ammunition ship crammed with explosives. One of them was a telegraph operator. He sent this message: "Ammunition ship on fire, drifting to Pier 9. Goodbye." His body was never found.

When the *Mont Blanc* exploded, a blizzard of metal, glass and wood fragments ripped through Halifax, mowing down everyone in its path. Many of the 6000 injured were blinded by the flying fragments.

Snow covering the devastated city after the explosion.

As a huge mushroom cloud formed in the sky, shock waves flattened almost all the buildings and homes of Halifax.

Pieces of the *Mont Blanc* fell all over the city and in the surrounding countryside. An anchor fell to earth five kilometres from the blast. A steel door landed four kilometres in the other direction. A fully-clothed sailor was hurled so far into the air that he landed on a hillside two kilometres away, unhurt — but wearing only his boots, his clothes torn off by the blast. For a few moments the bottom of Halifax harbour could be seen, all the water momentarily blown out of it.

Over a million square metres of Halifax were destroyed. A barn 40 kilometres away was blown off its foundations. Ships far out at sea felt the jolt of the blast and feared they had been torpedoed.

To make matters worse, soon after the explosion a freezing winter storm descended on the mutilated city and covered it with a blanket of snow. Many of the homeless had to endure hours of miserable cold before they could find shelter.

Ships loaded with coffins, medical supplies and tents rushed to the port, while determined survivors immediately started repairing the damage. Telephone and telegraph lines were reconnected. Power was restored and the injured were tended to.

Later, many of the victims of the explosion helped rebuild their city with pride. As a result of the disaster, Halifax became one of Canada's most modern cities, the first to be designed beforehand.

Years after the explosion, a court of law decided the *Imo* was mostly responsible for the disaster.

8
A Hurricane That Couldn't Happen

Most Canadians feel they are safe from the weather inside their homes. It's hard to imagine a storm so bad that your house is turned into a death trap! People living in the southeastern United States or in the Caribbean know what such weather is like, but people in Toronto don't expect it to happen to them.

They certainly didn't believe it would happen in 1954, even when they were warned. But they found out otherwise when a hurricane passed through Toronto, killing 81 people and destroying millions of dollars worth of property.

Hurricane Hazel began near Granada in the Caribbean. It was the eighth hurricane of 1954, and by far the biggest. Its circling winds covered an area 1500 kilometres wide and sent heavy rainfall and screaming winds to the island of Haiti and the American southeast coast.

Then, after 10 days, it made an unusual hop over

The remains of a bridge after the hurricane.

the Adirondak Mountains and crossed Lake Ontario to hit Toronto full force on October 15, catching almost everybody off guard. There had been warnings on the radio, but it just didn't seem possible. Hurricanes were for places like Florida, not Toronto.

It struck near midnight. Its winds weren't as strong as they had been, but it still carried huge amounts of water, and that was deadly. The hurricane dropped 18 centimetres of rain in a 24 hour period, more water than ever before in that length of time. Already rain had been falling for weeks, and the whole area around Toronto was soggy. The ground was like a full sponge which just couldn't hold any more.

Since the billions of litres of water dropped by Hurricane Hazel couldn't soak into the ground, it all flowed downhill, flooding ditches, creeks and rivers. Each swollen ditch emptied into a racing creek, and each creek poured into a monster river. Soon the rivers were higher than they had ever been, higher than the highest spring flood levels. And they kept getting bigger. The Humber overflowed its banks and began to look more like a fast-moving lake than a river. The Don River, the Rouge River, Highland Creek and Black Creek all turned into raging torrents of brown water with currents so fast that the best swimmers in the world would be swept along like chips of wood. Many of the rivers and creeks were up to three metres deeper than normal. Imagine water from floor to ceiling roaring through a creek bed!

The first casualties were the bridges, even those built to resist the powerful waters of spring floods. Twenty-four of the 28 bridges in the affected area were totally wrecked. Next, water began to find its way into houses. Many people woke on that Friday night to find their living rooms flooded, or water halfway up the stairs. Some didn't even have a chance to leave their beds before the water picked their houses up and floated them along on the incredible currents.

A housekeeping problem for a Toronto resident after Hurricane Hazel.

On Raymore Drive, all the houses on one bend were lifted from their foundations and swept away by the racing waters of the Humber River. Firefighters and police officers lined the banks and tried to throw ropes to helpless victims standing on houses and cars and in trees. The rising waters reached many before the ropes did, and it wasn't until days later that their bodies were found farther downstream. At one flooded bridge, rescue workers tried to talk a man out of driving his car across. They knew he wouldn't make it. But the man insisted. The car was lifted off the bridge and taken bobbing along on the water, the man and his family screaming for help. They all perished.

Eight firefighters were called to rescue people trapped in a car on another street near the Humber River. They hurried to the scene, only to find the people long gone. Then the fire truck itself was caught by the water and the firefighters had to climb on top of it. Nervously they watched the water rise. When it began to roll the fire truck over, the men jumped and tried to swim for shore. Only three of them made it.

In another trouble spot a firefighter named Norm Elwin singlehandedly lifted and extended an 11 metre ladder to some people trapped in a house. After the storm, others tried to duplicate his feat. None could. It took at least four men in normal conditions to do what Norm Elwin did alone during the hurricane.

The storm left behind terrible destruction and misery. If a hurricane is predicted for the Toronto area in the future, you can be sure people will listen. They learned their lesson in 1954.

9
The Killer Storm

If a ship sinks in a storm, that in itself is a disaster. If two or three ships go down in the same storm, then the disaster is that much more tragic. Imagine, then, the extent of the calamity when 30 ships went down and 235 sailors were lost on the weekend of November 7-9, 1913, in the worst storm in Canada's history.

This tragedy occurred not in the freezing, iceberg-dotted Atlantic Ocean, nor off the rocky coast of the Pacific. It took place on the fresh blue waters of Lake Huron.

Sailors on the oceans like to make fun of Great Lakes sailors. They believe that only on the high seas are you a true sailor, facing real dangers and storms. But they are sadly mistaken. Every year in the late fall the Great Lakes produce some of nature's deadliest storms.

November is always a bad month. The winter freeze-up is near, the shipping season is almost over, and the hard-working sailors are impatient to be home with their families. A walk on the open deck from forward to aft can chill you to the bone.

The November storms, which happen every season, are the worst trial of all. But most ships' captains try to push their freighters through them, since each completed trip represents thousands of dollars of revenue. The storms come and the ships survive, year in, year out. If a storm is too severe, a ship can always take shelter in the lee of an island or a point and let the land block the wind. Sometimes a storm is so bad a ship can be driven ashore, dragging its anchors behind it.

That year, the week before November 7 produced the usual warnings about the probability of severe storms on Lake Huron. While families huddled around stoves in Collingwood, Goderich and Owen Sound, men and ships pushed into the growing storm. Freezing water made the ships heavy and hard to steer as it covered them like frosting on a cake. For many sailors this was the last run of the season. For others it would be the last run of their lives.

The *James C. Carruthers*, Canada's newest ship, had made only three trips since sliding into the water in the Collingwood shipyards. It was one of the longest ships on the Great Lakes, equal in length to

The *Wexford* in dry dock before she was lost in the Lake Huron storm.

one and a half football fields, and its proud captain wasn't about to let a storm slow him down.

But this storm would stop him cold. On Friday night the weather began to deteriorate. Ships near land dropped anchor because the snow was so thick that visibility was reduced to just a few metres. Freighters in the middle of the lake cautiously steered by compass, since radar hadn't yet been invented and very few ships were equipped with the recently invented radio devices.

The waves rose and began to pound the ships. Hatch covers were knocked off and deck houses damaged. Captains had to run with the waves or steer against them. Any other course would roll a big ship over. As the weather deteriorated further, ship after ship dropped anchor and tried to fight the onrush of water. Gradually the winds — blowing at 100 kilometres an hour — pushed many vessels onto rocky shores. Some dragged their anchors behind them, their engines at "full speed ahead" while the winds drove them relentlessly backward.

Still the weather worsened. Other ships, farther out, began to break up under the relentless pounding. Some simply rolled over, throwing shouting sailors into the cold grey lake.

The *Wexford*, built years before in the finest British shipyards, sank with all hands. It had survived the worst weather ever seen on the oceans, but succumbed to this Lake Huron storm. The *James C. Carruthers* went to the bottom late Friday night. The *Regina*, another Canadian ship, disappeared without a trace. American ships like the *Charles S. Price*, the *Isaac M. Scott* and the *Argus* were also lost in the storm and never seen again. A lightship (a floating lighthouse) was driven ashore by the waves. Many other ships, steering by its light, ran aground as well.

Captains reported that at the height of the storm the waves came in groups of three and the wind changed direction frequently. Sometimes it blew crosswise to the waves, making steering the

The *Regina*, one of the freighters that was lost with all hands.

ice-encrusted ships almost impossible. The storm was at its most intense for 12 long hours throughout Friday night. Even after that, the shrieking wind and icy waves continued through the whole of Saturday and Sunday. Finally the wind and waves died down and bodies began floating ashore along the Ontario coastline of Lake Huron.

Who can say exactly what happened during those long, drawn-out hours? From eight ships not a man lived to tell. The bodies that were recovered raised unanswerable questions. Crew members from an American ship were washed ashore in lifejackets from the Canadian vessel *Wexford*. A stewardess from the *Argus* floated ashore wearing the engineer's greatcoat and the captain's lifejacket. What tales of rescue, courage and self-sacrifice are left untold?

A memorial gravestone in Goderich stands above the spot where five unidentified seamen lie buried. A single word is inscribed on it: *SAILORS*.

10
The Lost Race of Indians

One of the greatest tragedies in Canada was the loss of an entire race of native people. The Beothuk Indians of Newfoundland died out completely after trying to share the land with the European settlers of the 1600's. Before Europeans came to Canada, different bands of native people lived throughout the country, each with its own language and customs. One of these groups was the Beothuk tribe of Newfoundland.

There have been many stories about the Beothuks. Some say they were white-skinned, blond giants who were so gentle they wouldn't protect themselves from aggressors. There were also supposed to be 50 000 of them living before the English and Irish came to tend their nets on the Newfoundland shores. But modern research tells a different story. There were probably never more than 1000, judging by the number of villages they built.

Though some of them were very tall, most were about the same height as the Europeans of the time. Evidence indicates they did have light skin and different hair colours. This suggests they probably mixed with Viking visitors in earlier times. Their language was similar to the Algonkian Indian languages. They were excellent hunters and trappers. And they covered everything — themselves and all their tools — with a red dye. It is probably because of the Beothuks that the term "Red Indians" became popular.

When Europeans first came to Newfoundland, their contacts with the Beothuks were friendly, but the friendship soon went bad. A British ship's captain fired at a group of Beothuks one spring when he feared they were going to attack his vessel. It turned out they were coming out in their canoes to welcome him. A few years later, Beothuks killed two English soldiers because they thought they were about to be lured into a trap. The soldiers were just trying to make friends.

There is a terrible story about a whole band of Beothuks who were herded onto a point of land and then slaughtered one by one by a group of fishermen. The story might be true. There definitely were trappers who shot at Beothuks and even bragged about how they hunted them like deer.

Some well-known Canadian writers claim that whole towns of Newfoundland residents hunted the Beothuks for sport, but there is no proof for such tales and they are probably not true. On the contrary, there were long periods when English settlers and Beothuk Indians lived peacefully within a few kilometres of each other. But then, when the English trappers moved inland with their guns, dogs and fishing nets, the Beothuks really began to suffer. The newcomers caught most of the fish and shot all the bear and caribou, and the Beothuk hunters and their families went hungry.

In an attempt to make the invaders leave their forest, the Beothuks stole the trappers' supplies and destroyed their boats and guns. In retaliation the trappers tracked down Beothuk settlements, took back their supplies and burned the villages to the ground. Both sides were determined to survive. The Beothuks stole supplies from under the very noses of the settlers, sometimes watching from treetops and waiting all day for a chance, and the English trappers, with their deadly guns, got back at the Indians by shooting them. After all, stealing in those days was punished by hanging, so they felt they were right. Laws were made that said the two sides had to keep away from each other, but the lawmakers and enforcers were in England, too far away to be of any use. The only time the trappers obeyed was when an

English ship lay at anchor. Otherwise people did what they thought was right.

Large numbers of Beothuks began to sicken and die, partly because they weren't getting enough to eat. They were used to eating meat all through the winter, and now it was scarce. They were also being exposed to the diseases the white people brought with them from Europe. They had never come up against such diseases before and their bodies were not equipped to fight them off the way the newcomers could.

The British Government started to worry about the Beothuks. They realized that if the fighting and bad feelings went on there would soon be no Indians left at all, so they made plans to save the tribe. They decided to lure the Beothuks away from the forest and close to the town of St. John's, where they could be protected. But instead of setting up a reserve where white men wouldn't be allowed to go, they came up with the idea of capturing a few Beothuks, teaching them to be like Europeans and then sending them back among their own people to teach the others to be like Europeans too!

A government party set out into the woods and came upon a Beothuk camp, where they captured the wife of the chief. She couldn't run away fast enough because she was carrying a sick baby. The chief, a giant of a man, came forward to protest. He made it

Shanawdithit (Nancy)

Last survivor of Beothucks so far as is known. Captured in 1823, died in St John's, 1829.

quite clear he wouldn't allow them to take his wife away, and tried to pull her back, ignoring the English guns. When the soldiers refused to let go of her, he attacked with his bare hands. After a bloody fight, the Beothuk chief was killed.

The woman was named Mary March and taken back to St. John's. She was miserable there, even though she was treated like a princess and given anything she needed. She lived in St. John's for two years before she died of tuberculosis. Other Beothuks were captured and taken to live with the English settlers, but they all contracted European diseases and died.

The last living Beothuck was named Shanawdithit, but the English called her Nancy. She was one of three sick and starving women who sought help from a white trapper. The other two died soon after they were taken in, but Shanawdithit survived and was taken to St. John's, where she worked as a servant. She was a bright woman, as was shown by the sketches she made of Beothuk life. But nobody studied or recorded what she had to say, though she could have explained much about the Beothuks. She did say that when Mary March was captured there were only 27 Beothuks left, many of them sick. Now her few sketches are all that is left of the Beothuk people. Shanawdithit died in 1829, in her 30's. With her died a whole race of people.

11
The Mysterious Crash of Flight 831

On November 29, 1963, a Trans-Canada Airlines jet dove into a hillside at Ste. Thérèse-de-Blainville in Quebec, instantly killing all 118 on board.

It was raining hard in Montreal when the big DC-8 taxied to the takeoff runway at Dorval Airport. Flight 831 was a routine one, filled with businessmen flying to Toronto at suppertime. The regular pilot was late flying into Montreal that particular night, so Captain John Snider took his place on the doomed jet. Snider knew as much about the DC-8 as any pilot in the world. The co-pilot and flight engineer were also well acquainted with the comparatively new jet. But all their combined knowledge and experience couldn't save them that rainy Friday night.

Eight people cursed in frustration when the plane roared down the runway, upset by the fact that heavy traffic had caused them to miss their flight. The takeoff was normal. The plane's four jet engines

Investigators search through the wreckage of the doomed DC-8.

pushed it up into the rainstorm, each gulping down jet fuel and air and blasting out 8000 kilos of thrust. At 1000 metres, the co-pilot reported to Dorval that everything was as it should be. That was the last report the crew sent. Something happened before the plane reached 2000 metres, the next regular check-in point. It might have been a powerful air current, or perhaps a faulty instrument in the cockpit. No one knows why, but for some reason the 50 metre long aircraft was suddenly diving for the ground at full speed.

When a jet as large as a DC-8 goes into a dive, it reaches such high speeds so quickly that thousands of metres are needed to slow the plane and bring it up. If it is pulled out too quickly the wings can be torn off. Flight 831 hadn't yet reached an altitude where those extra metres were available. The pilots did the best they could. They tried desperately to pull the plane up, but it screamed into a hillside killing all aboard. The impact shook the ground so hard that people living nearby wondered if they were experiencing an earthquake.

A column of smoke led people to the area of the crash. All they found were a few pieces of twisted metal. Today, specially-built machines encased in strong, crash-proof boxes record every movement of an aircraft and every word spoken by the crew, but in 1963 flight recorders weren't required in Canadian aircraft. So there is no record of what happened in those few final seconds. The secret of this crash lies with the dead.

12
The Night the Mountain Fell

In 1903 the town of Frank, Alberta, was a noisy
mining community. Many single men slept in tents
at night and worked at the coal face during the day.
They drifted into town, worked a while, spent their
money and drifted out again. Very few records were
ever kept, so nobody knows exactly how many
drifters pitched their tents in the town. But neat
square houses provided homes for nearly 1000
permanent residents. Most of the husbands and
fathers worked in the mine too.

Frank was built beneath a large white mountain
called Turtle Mountain, which local Indians would
never camp under. They said that someday the big
turtle-shaped triangle of limestone at the top would
"nod its head" and roll down the mountain. The local
townspeople thought that was ridiculous, but they
ended up thinking differently.

It was April 29, 1903. On the "graveyard" shift

The town of Frank nestled beneath Turtle Mountain before the slide.

(from midnight to 8:00 a.m.) a small group of men went deep into the mine. One of them noticed that the horse was nervous. It made him worry about a cave-in, because animals seem to be able to sense such things more easily than people do. But nothing happened, and the men worked busily, hour after hour. In town, things quietened down. The bars closed and by 4:00 a.m. most of the residents of the town were asleep.

Then it happened. Half of the white mountain high above the town broke loose. A gigantic slab of limestone, weighing about 60 million tonnes, broke into boulders the size of houses and buses, and these came crashing down the mountainside, crushing and pulverizing everything before them. The homes and other buildings in one whole section of Frank were flattened as if they were made of paper. On and on the boulders bounced and crashed, covering the wide valley floor and rolling halfway up the other side of the valley. In just a minute and a half more than 100 people and their homes or tents were buried to the depth of a 10-storey building.

In some houses right on the edge of the path of destruction, one half of the home was pulverized and the other half was left standing. All the people sleeping in one room were killed, those in the next untouched. Boards, pipes and roof beams lay scattered with the rocks as far as the eye could see. The Old Man River and the CPR tracks lay buried under 30 metres of rock.

A man named Sid Choquette was the hero of the night. He worked for the CPR and knew there was a night train due at any moment. He raced across the hot, broken rocks of the slide and flagged it down before it reached the area of devastation. If he hadn't succeeded in his desperate effort the train would have crashed straight into the rocks, taking even more lives.

A number of people had some lucky escapes. Perhaps the luckiest was Marion Leitch. She was just a baby in a crib when the boulders crushed her house

After the slide.

like a cardboard box. She was thrown into the air on impact and would have landed hard on a huge rock if a pile of hay hadn't landed on the same rock just moments before she did. She landed as gently as if she had been playfully tossed onto a bed. Marion survived, along with her sisters. But her brothers and parents all perished.

Almost as lucky as Marion was the group of miners. The entrance to the mine was buried under tonnes of rock. They dug for hours with their mining tools, none of them realizing that this was anything more than just a cave-in of the mine close to the entrance. Finally one of the men was pushed out through the hole they had dug. William Warrington stood blinking in the bright sunlight. He stared, unbelieving, at the pile of broken rocks that covered the whole valley. His happiness at escaping the mine's dark trap turned to sorrow when he saw that the rocks covered what had been his home, with his wife and daughters inside.

In the years that followed, the town of Frank was rebuilt a few kilometres away. Nobody wanted to live beneath Turtle Mountain. Today, visitors can see the jumble of rocks stretching across the valley. Beneath, still buried, lie many victims of the Frank Slide.

13
The Nightmare of a "Safe" Drug

Imagine not being able to shake hands or throw a ball or walk properly. Simple things like these are difficult, if not impossible, for about 80 Canadians who were born in 1961 and 1962. They have birth defects caused by a drug their mothers took before they were born. The drug had been advertised as safe to take.

Phocomelia is the name of a deformity which can occur during the early stages of the development of an unborn child. The word means "flipper-like." Legs or arms don't develop completely, so that a hand grows from an elbow or a shoulder, or a foot grows from a hip, looking like a flipper. Before 1958, many doctors had never seen a person with phocomelia. But in the late 1950's and early 1960's, doctors all over the world recorded more and more cases of this and other birth defects. Some babies were born without any arms or legs at all. In Canada, 121 children were

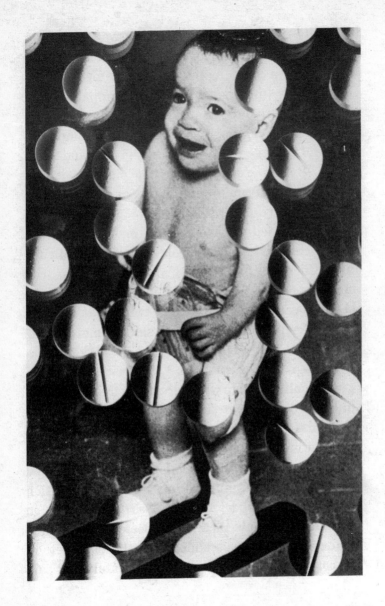

born with defects. Many of them died at birth.

The cause was a drug called thalidomide. It was invented by a company in Germany named Chemie Grunenthal. In Canada, two drug companies sold thalidomide under their own brand names of Kevadon and Talimol. The Canadian companies were told the inventors had tested the drug and found it safe. It was used as a sleeping pill, and it also stopped people from feeling nauseous. Most doctors never give any drugs to a pregnant woman, unless they are needed to save her life or the life of her unborn child. It is one of the oldest rules in medicine. But Chemie Grunenthal announced in its advertisements that thalidomide was non-toxic, meaning it couldn't poison you, even if you took too much. Even aspirin isn't that safe. Some doctors, believing the advertisements, gave thalidomide to their pregnant patients.

Actually, doctors who were given free samples of thalidomide in the late 1950's had already discovered problems with it long before its effect on unborn children was known. There were some doctors who found that their patients developed something called peripheral neuritis after taking the drug, a condition in which the fingers or toes lose feeling and go permanently numb. When these doctors told Chemie Grunenthal what was happening, the managers of the company wrote to each one separately and said they had never heard of such problems before. Each doctor thought his patient was the only one suffering from peripheral neuritis after taking thalidomide, and decided that the cause of the problem must be something else.

Eventually, doctors realized that the mothers of all the deformed babies being born had taken thalidomide during their pregnancies. The drug was quickly taken off the shelves of pharmacies and banned from sale. But the damage had been done. For months, babies continued to be born with external and internal defects caused by this "safe" drug. Some doctors who had prescribed thalidomide couldn't stand to face their patients and moved to other cities.

In Canada, about 80 people born with these defects have lived difficult lives. Some have slight problems, like webbed fingers or toes; but others struggle to use artificial limbs to do the simplest things. Next time you hold hands, dance or run, think how lucky you are.

14
The Nightmare That Almost Came True

On the night of June 16, 1958, Gary Poirier had a nightmare. He dreamed that the bridge he was helping to build collapsed and that he was cut in half by a steel cable as he fell. The next morning Gary was nervous when he went to work on the new Second Narrows Bridge in Vancouver. It was being built to replace the old bridge, which joined the city of Vancouver to North Vancouver on the other side of Burrard Inlet.

It was a warm and sunny day, and the other high-steel construction workers were in a good mood, walking back and forth on steel beams just 15 centimetres wide. Gary tried to forget his dream, but he couldn't. The section of the bridge he was working on was a long span hanging out over the water of the inlet. Like the other workers, Gary wore a bright yellow lifejacket. A man in a rowboat waited below to rescue anyone who might accidentally fall.

The Second Narrows Bridge after the collapse.

Suddenly, at 3:40 p.m., there were two loud cracks, like rifle shots, and the farthest span, the one Gary was working on, dropped toward the water. Some of the men hung on with all their strength. Others jumped, pushing themselves out as far from the falling steel as possible.

The whole span fell the height of a 15-storey building before plunging into the water. It pulled a concrete pillar out of place, sending the next span and the men working on it crashing down as well. Those who were wearing heavy tool belts plummeted through the water until they touched bottom. Others

61

were trapped by the steel beams and killed. Still others rode the girders down like cowboys, jumping off at the right moment. Gary fell exactly as he had in his dream, but he wasn't cut in half. He was one of the lucky ones who lived.

George Schmidt landed on top of a steel girder just above the water. When he noticed that one of his legs had been cut off below the knee, he calmly tied his work belt around it to stop the bleeding, lit a cigarette and waited to be rescued. "Thanks, fellas," was all he said when he was picked up.

Boats came from everywhere to help rescue the men, some of whom had to be cut free from the twisted wreckage. In all, 18 people died. An investigation later claimed that the accident was the result of a mathematical error. But the two engineers who are thought to have made the mistake were killed in the collapse, so their story can never be told. The Second Narrows Bridge was eventually opened two years later, in 1960. The ribbon was cut by one of the survivors of the earlier collapse.

15
The *Noronic* Fire

In 1949, the *SS Noronic* was the biggest and best ship on the Great Lakes. But in that year a needless fire destroyed the $3.5 million ship and took the lives of 118 passengers.

The *Noronic*, owned by Canada Steamship Lines, could carry almost 600 passengers. Over 100 metres long, it had five decks and several fine restaurants and bars. The *Noronic* was very popular as a tour boat on all the Great Lakes.

It was also a death trap. Today such a ship would never be allowed to carry passengers, and sailors would refuse to sign aboard it. Although the hull and decks were made of steel, everything else was made of wood. Yet there was no sprinkler system and many of the fire hoses didn't work. And even though the *Noronic's* sister ship, the *Hamonic*, had been destroyed in a blaze just four years earlier, the sailors on the *Noronic* weren't properly instructed in fire control.

A victim of the fire being taken off the ship.

In September, 1949, nobody knew that the beautiful big ship was about to become a sad page in history. On the 17th, the ship tied up at Pier 9 in Toronto. At about 1:15 a.m., a small fire broke out in a closet where maids hid to smoke cigarettes. A passenger and a porter found the fire and tried to put it out, but the nearest fire hose wouldn't work. By the time an alarm was sent to the Toronto fire department, the blaze was out of control. The fire had raced along a passenger hallway and smoke was rapidly filling the ship. Sleepy passengers,

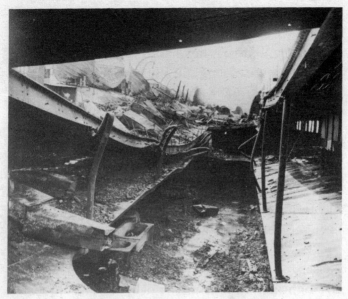

The burnt-out hulk of the *Noronic*.

frightened by the smoke, panicked and ran in all directions. The dry, painted wood burned like kindling.

On the bow of the *Noronic* some women tried to climb down ladders onto the dock. A few men started to push them aside so they could go down first. Two brothers, Art and Gordon Alves, pitched the men into the black water and let the women go ahead. Also in the bow, two little sisters waited calmly while many adults around them panicked. Art Alves found six-year-old Barbara Kerr waiting and told her to ride piggy back while he climbed down a rope. Her eight-year-old sister climbed down a glowing-hot steel cable, burning her hands, but saving her own life. They were among the 500 lucky passengers who survived the fire.

At some point an officer turned on the main foghorn and it blew with an insane shrieking all through the night. People jumped into the water and drowned trying to escape the flaming death on the ship. One hundred and eighteen people are known to have died in the fire, though only 104 bodies were ever recovered. The ship itself was a total loss.

Laws were made soon after to ensure that all passenger ships had sprinkler systems and fire-fighting equipment which worked properly. Nobody wanted to be responsible for another fire like the one which destroyed the *Noronic*. Now only the foghorn is left, made dull and old-looking by the heat of the fire. It sits on display in the Marine Museum of Toronto. When it blows its low, sad note, you can almost feel the flames and panic of September 17, 1949.

16
The Regina Tornado

Imagine a wind so strong it can lift you up and carry you through the air! The winds in a tornado can do just this, lifting people, cars and houses as if they were nothing at all. A tornado is a small circular storm that looks like a dark funnel coming out of a black thundercloud. Its spinning winds can explode houses, tear buildings apart and leave a trail of wreckage in any neighbourhood.

In 1912, on June 30, a tornado hit Regina, Saskatchewan. It cut a long path of destruction through the young city, taking almost everybody by surprise. In Saskatchewan tornadoes are very rare, but when two dark clouds collided over the Queen City on that Dominion Day weekend, many people got first-hand experience of their devasting power.

The tornado formed above Wascana Lake and sucked the water up into a long green spout. Several boaters were drawn up with the water and killed.

A Regina street after the tornado.

There was one, however, who had a miraculous escape. He was a 13-year-old boy who was picked up in his canoe and spun through the air for over a kilometre, only to land gently, far from the water with nothing worse than a broken arm.

When the tornado moved on across the land, people, houses and horses were lifted into the dark funnel and whirled around at speeds of more than 100 kilometres an hour. In some places buildings were totally destroyed while those just across the street merely lost their windows. Other buildings lost whole walls, revealing the interiors of offices and apartments to anyone who cared to look. Among the surprised people suddenly exposed to the world like this were some sitting down to dinner and one taking a bath. Three large churches were completely destroyed. A fourth, left unharmed, was the only one with people in it when the tornado struck.

Most of the windows of the new Saskatchewan Legislative Building were blown out and much of its copper roof was sent flying off into the prairie. The examination papers for all the province's public schools had been stacked neatly on tables in one of the exposed offices. The tornado answered the prayers of thousands of students when it scattered the papers like leaves on a fall day. No student in Saskatchewan had to write final exams that year.

Just as suddenly as it began, the tornado left the city and disappeared. Many people had been killed and hundreds were left wounded. Dozens were trapped in fallen buildings or scarred by flying objects. A 15-year-old girl who went outside just after the storm ended remarked on the silence. Those trapped or wounded hardly made a sound. Instead they waited quietly to be rescued. There was even some good-natured joking as people lay piled on top of each other in dark basements or the remains of stores or apartments.

Slowly the extent of the damage became clear. Here was the roof of a house. Fifty metres away was one of its outside walls. On one street a bed, hardly rumpled, sat waiting to be claimed. Its owner lived three blocks away. There was amazing evidence of the fierce power of the storm. Straws of grass had been hurled through the air so hard that they were found embedded in tree trunks. Boards had smashed into brick walls with such force that they stuck out like porcupine quills.

Many people had miraculous escapes. A boy tried to hold onto his baby sister while their house collapsed around them, but she was torn from his arms. Later she was found in the oven of the kitchen stove with only a few bruises on her legs. A woman and her baby fell through the top two floors of their house and landed in the basement, completely unhurt. In one office building a bookkeeper had been using the holiday to catch up on his work. He went into the company vault to get some ledgers and when he came out he found the building had collapsed all around him. On a street corner a rooster was crowing as loudly as he could. All his feathers were missing except those on his tail.

Rebuilding the city began immediately. Repairs to the essential services were the first priority. The province lent money, and many nearby cities gave tents and lumber to help the people who had lost their homes. Officers of the North West Mounted Police were called in to stand guard over the valuables and furniture which still lay scattered all over the city. Military troops and boy scouts were also called in to help in whatever ways they could.

These days people know what to do if a tornado is near: stay as low to the ground as possible and open a few windows. The inside of a tornado has no air pressure, and if one passes over or near a building with all the windows shut the lack of pressure can cause the building to explode outwards.

Though some people in Regina called their tornado a cyclone, "tornado" is actually the more accurate word. Each year tornadoes occur farther and farther north. The possibility of another Regina tornado gets stronger all the time.

17
Slow Death

"I worked with 180 men on that job and there's 142 of them in the graveyard."

Sammy Byrne, a Newfoundland fluorspar miner.

When the fluorspar mine opened in St. Lawrence, Newfoundland, in 1957, it seemed like a gift from God. Four years of poor catches had left the people of the fishing village sickly, underfed and weak, with children dying of diseases they would otherwise have been able to fight off. The new mine seemed to hold the solution to these problems. Since fluorspar is used in the production of steel and aluminum, there would be a steady demand for the mineral. And although mining would be at least as dangerous as fishing, the work would be available all year and the pay would be steady.

The fishermen knew nothing about mining, since none of them had ever worked in a mine before.

So they didn't know that most mines are equipped with two entry shafts, one for the men and ore to get in and out, the other for fresh-air ventilation and, if necessary, emergency escape. The St. Lawrence mine had only one shaft. Fresh air was forced into it, but the air's circulation was limited and not much of it reached the miners. In addition, the men were given "dry hammer" drills to use. These drills create clouds of dry, choking dust because, unlike "wet" drills, they don't have water running through the middle of the drill steel.

The men worked hard, unaware that they were working in one of the dustiest mines in North America. Mine bosses inspected the mine on Sundays, when the dust had settled. There were also problems with the nitrogen gases left over from explosions. The common practice in other mines was to wait a half-hour after a blasting for the poisonous gases to clear, but these directions weren't given to the miners here. Sometimes the gases were too much for a miner and he would collapse. After he revived, he went back to work. Miners from other areas who came to work at St. Lawrence quit when they discovered what the conditions were like.

But the worst and most dangerous aspect of the mine was invisible. Deadly radiation was leaking from a large deposit of uranium nearby. The terrible thing about radiation poisoning is that its effects may not become apparent for months or even years after exposure.

Gradually, more and more miners came down with mysterious ailments, and then they began to die, one by one. The sick were sent to a hospital in St. John's, but seldom were they told what their illnesses were, or what was causing them. Finally, a company doctor did reveal the truth. Many of the sick men were suffering from cancer. Others had silicosis, a deadly disease of the lungs which afflicts miners. Such diseases were caused by the unwholesome conditions of the mine, the doctor explained, and within two weeks he was looking for another job.

In 1960, the Alcan Corporation purchased the mine from its American owners. They dug another shaft to ventilate it properly and replaced the dry hammers with wet drills, and the dust problem diminished. But disease was already creeping through the bodies of many of the workers. By the early 1970's one family in three had lost a man.

Many had to go on welfare. Others applied to the company for compensation, but they received so little that they could barely keep their families fed and clothed. The miners couldn't understand why compensation varied from one person to another. A man who was "one quarter disabled" received less than one who was "half disabled," and he in turn received less than one who was "two thirds disabled." The issue seemed straightforward to the miners: either a man is disabled or he isn't.

Men dying of lung cancer continued to work to earn a few dollars more for their families. Some refused to leave until they barely had enough strength to walk. The fluorspar mines in Newfoundland closed in February, 1978.

18
The Springhill Mine Disaster: 1891

On February 21, 1891, 121 miners were killed in an explosion in the Cumberland mine in Springhill, Nova Scotia. Twelve of them were under 16 years old. It was the worst mine disaster in Canada. Joseph Dupee was only 12 years old when he died in the explosion; his friends Peter Reid and Willard Carter were only 13. In those days there were no laws to prevent children from working. If a family was poor, the children simply had to work, often for only a few cents an hour. There was no welfare or unemployment insurance. Neither were there any safety laws. The men and boys relied on instinct and common sense to keep themselves alive in the mine tunnels.

Every day the boys would put on stiff, dusty mining clothes, take their lunch pails and lanterns and walk to the mine. Once in the mine they would

A 14-YEAR-OLD WORKER IN A COAL MINE.
Is this the best modern civilization can do for
our boys?

walk another kilometre or so through the tunnels until they reached their workplaces. Springhill was thought to be one of the safest mines in Nova Scotia at the time, though this didn't stop the miners from worrying about accidents. On February 19, an inspector made a routine tour of the mine and declared everything to be in order. Two days later, disaster struck. An explosion ripped through the air, which was full of coal dust that flared like burning gas.

Everyone close to the explosion was killed instantly, and lamps throughout the mine were blown out by the blast. Many miners survived the flash fire only to succumb to a deadly white gas called "afterdamp." This gas, which often appears in the wake of such fires, collected in low spots and choked the men as they desperately scrambled to safety.

There were many acts of heroism that day in the life-and-death struggle which followed the explosion. A badly burned 14-year-old boy carried a young friend to safety on his back. Young men and old braved the afterdamp to go down into the mine to help. One rescuer had to be carried from the mine in shock when he found the bodies of three of his sons. Again and again the rescuers descended into the darkness to help the survivors.

An investigation found that there was too much

coal dust in the air, so the investigating committee recommended that the dusty areas be wetted down more frequently!

Springhill regained its reputation as a safe place to work, and retained it until a day in 1956 . . .

19
The Springhill Mine Disaster: 1956

The second Springhill mine disaster occurred on February 1, 1956. A train of ore cars went out of control and flew for thousands of metres down the smooth steel tracks before derailing.

The sparks caused a massive blast and fire which killed 39 miners. Another 88 were trapped underground and were thought to be dead. But then, three and a half days later, they were found alive and rescued. They were famous all over the world as the survivors of the "Springhill Miracle."

The mining company wanted to close the mine, but the people of Springhill were anxious that it stay open. The men couldn't stand the thought of losing their livelihood and being forced to collect welfare or unemployment, so the mine stayed open, but only until the third and final disaster in 1958.

Friends and relatives wait anxiously for news outside number four mine.

20
The Springhill Mine Disaster: 1958

On Thursday, October 23, 1958, 75 men died in a cave-in at the number two mine in Springhill. Nineteen other men were given up for dead, only to be rescued after being trapped underground for eight days.

The number two mine was the largest in North America. Its tunnels crept more than three kilometres down into the earth, following several seams of coal. At 8:06 p.m. on October 23, a sudden collapse of ground, called a "bump" by miners, flattened large sections of the mine and 75 miners were killed. The bump was so strong that scientists many kilometres away thought they had recorded an earthquake on their seismographs.

It wasn't long before practically the whole town was milling around the entrance shaft to number two mine. Rescue workers ignored the possibility of more bumps or flash fires or poisonous gases to go down into the depths to help the survivors. Seventy-two miners were brought out the first night. The rescuers also found the bodies of the less fortunate — and that large sections of the mine were totally blocked off by cave-ins. Newspaper reporters from all over the world waited with the anxious families of the missing miners. People remembered the Springhill miracle of 1956. The queen, the prime minister, and many prominent citizens sent telegrams to express their concern for the men trapped so far from the sun. Everyone hoped for another miracle.

Rescue workers put in eight-hour shifts around the clock as they dug through the caved-in tunnels in search of trapped men. Days passed. The people of Springhill buried their dead and the rescuers dug on. They worked steadily, but as the days went by and no more miners were found alive, hope for those still missing began to dwindle. Even the mine captain believed there was little point in continuing the search.

Then, after six and a half days, 12 desperate miners were found alive, trapped in a space so small they could only lie flat. One of them had shouted into a 20 metre long pipe at the exact moment that rescuers passed the other end. Word flashed through the community that more men had been found alive in the mine. Tearful families waited at the entrance as their loved ones were brought out one by one.

A miner is brought out of number two mine.

The rescue workers continued to crawl and hack their way through one caved-in section after another, and two days later they came upon another seven men. This group had been kept in high spirits throughout their eight-day ordeal by a black man named Maurice Ruddick who sang to the others until his voice gave out. (Later, on an all-expenses-paid vacation in the United States, Maurice was unable to stay with his workmates because of his colour.) Finally, one other miner was found alive in a space no bigger than a grave.

Shortly after this third Springhill tragedy the mine was closed down, and it has remained closed ever since. Only a museum is left now where the people of Springhill, Nova Scotia, experienced three big disasters and many miraculous rescues.

21
Stairway of Death

It was a bright but cold Sunday on January 9, 1927. More than 1000 Montreal children lined up at the Laurier Palace Theatre on St. Catherines St. to see the afternoon movies. Although the law in those days said that children had to bring someone over the age of 16 with them, many didn't and managed to get in anyway.

Most of them paid a precious quarter for seats in the main part of the theatre, but for those who came early enough, seats in the balcony cost only 15¢. Often there were just not enough of these cheaper seats available to accommodate all the kids who wanted them, and many ended up standing in the aisles instead. The program usually consisted of a newsreel, several cartoons and two movies. It was a popular way to spend a Sunday afternoon.

On this particular Sunday, the movies were *Sparrows*, with Mary Pickford, and a comedy called *Get 'Em Young*. The show was going well. The kids were enjoying the comedy when suddenly a boy spotted a curl of smoke at his feet. "Le feu! Le feu!" he shouted, and immediately kids all around stood up to see. The adults in the theatre tried to prevent panic, but they couldn't stop a rush for the exits on both sides of the balcony.

Down below, on the main floor of the theatre, the children saw the flames and they too rushed for the exits. Smoke began to billow out along the ceiling, adding to the compulsion to get out into the clean winter air. But at the eastern exit of the balcony, where kids had been standing in the aisles, a tragedy began to unfold.

Just five short steps from the sidewalk some of the smaller children tripped in their haste and fell. Others crashed on top of them, and those behind tumbled down as well. In no time the whole stairway leading to safety was filled from top to bottom with a mass of fallen children, all struggling to get free.

Firefighters were quickly on the scene, but not even the strongest of them could pull individuals free from the tangled heap. The fact that there were two bends in the stairway didn't help. Soon smoke was pouring down over the children, adding to the chaos. Water was sprayed over the crush of bodies while holes were desperately chopped in the walls beside the stairway and underneath it.

Constable Albert Boisseau was off duty, but he happened to be near the theatre and was one of the first rescuers on the scene. Among the dead children he eventually carried out of the theatre was his eldest daughter, who was supposed to have been skating with friends. Later he learned that his other two children had also died, suffocated on the stairway. Another family, the Quintals of Joliette St., also lost three children in the disaster.

One of the firefighters, Alphage Arpin, was sick with fear when he arrived at the theatre. He knew his own son had gone there that day. He was unable to find him among either the living or the dead at the theatre, but was heartbroken when he later found him at the morgue where dozens of the victims had been taken.

One boy, Roger Frappier, could well have been among the dead had it not been for his quick thinking. He was close to the fire when it started and he soon saw that he would never be able to escape through the eastern exit. Instead, he jumped from the balcony to one of the aisles below. Although he was injured in the fall, he did escape with his life.

Altogether, 77 people died in the fire. Most of them were boys and girls between the ages of eight and 12. All of them died on the eastern stairway. Since that disaster, theatres have had to obey strict laws dealing with the age of children who are admitted, and people are no longer allowed to stand in the aisles.

22
Sunk in 14 Minutes

The sinking of the *Titanic* was the worst sea tragedy in history, but the loss of a Canadian ship in 1914 was just as tragic, though it has been almost completely forgotten.

The *Empress of Ireland* was a Canadian Pacific passenger liner built in 1906. After the *Titanic* tragedy, all passenger liners had to be fully equipped with lifeboats and lifejackets and their crews well trained in dealing with emergencies. But on the night of May 29, 1914, on the St. Lawrence Seaway just past Rimouski, Quebec, a disaster occurred in which all the training and all the life-saving equipment aboard couldn't prevent a terrible loss of life.

The *Storstad*, a Norwegian coal ship, fully laden and very heavy, was steaming upstream as the *Empress* headed downstream. A fog bank rolled in, so the ships couldn't see each other. Because radar

The *Empress of Ireland* before the fatal collision.

hadn't been invented yet, the captain of the *Empress* and the first mate of the *Storstad* both had to guess where the other ship was. Nobody can be sure just who was really at fault, but the mate of the *Storstad* was blamed for turning in the wrong direction in the fog. He claimed the *Empress* had turned in the wrong direction too.

Standing at the bridge, peering into the fog, Captain Kendall of the *Empress of Ireland* could only watch helplessly as the *Storstad* came looming out of the mist to ram his ship. The St. Lawrence River gushed into the enormous hole left by the *Storstad*,

The Norwegian coal ship *Storstad* after ramming the *Empress of Ireland* in the fog.

and the *Empress* quickly keeled over. The list on the ship prevented watertight doors from closing, so people in the lower-deck cabins were caught in their beds by the rushing water. Others woke in time, only to be caught in the crowded hallways. Water soon poured right into the boilers and the mighty engines died, and with them died all the lights and power. By now the ship was listing so badly that only the lifeboats on the side nearest the water could be lowered. In all the panic and pandemonium, sailors filled the boats with passengers and sent them out into the dark. Other passengers jumped into the near-freezing water with their lifejackets on. On board were 170 Salvation Army workers. They gave their own lifejackets to those who had none. Only 24 of them were alive the next day.

Nearby, the *Storstad* was still floating, its bow crumpled by the accident, its lifeboats in the water rescuing survivors from the *Empress*. Hundreds of cold, half-naked people were pulled from the water, too weak to move. Many others floated face down in the river, dead from the numbing cold. Other ships steamed to the rescue, but before they could arrive the *Empress of Ireland* rolled on her side and sank from view. Only 14 minutes had passed since she was hit.

The hero of the night was Doctor James Grant. Half frozen and half naked himself, no sooner was he pulled from the water and taken aboard the *Storstad* than he began reviving people and telling others how to help, as well as setting bones and comforting those beyond medical help. When a near-riot broke out between a group of people who all spoke different languages, he stopped the trouble unaided. While he was attending the chief engineer of the *Empress*, a half-crazed man barged in and threatened the doctor. Doctor Grant knocked the man out and continued with his work.

The St. Lawrence River claimed 1012 people that night, 840 of whom were passengers. Most of their bodies were never recovered. The wreck of the *Empress of Ireland* still lies at the bottom of the St. Lawrence in 50 metres of water. Even as you read this, ships are passing above her remains, the final resting place for hundreds of the victims of Canada's worst marine disaster.

23

A Terrible Mistake

Landing any plane, large or small, is the most difficult part of flying. Many things must be done quickly and smoothly, and all in a very short time.

Landing commercial passenger jets is particularly difficult. They have to land at high speeds and then slow down very quickly to avoid overshooting the runway. To help with this, they are equipped with large flaps on the wings called spoilers. When operated, they "spoil" the ability of the wings to lift the aircraft, and at the same time slow it down. They are designed to be used after the aircraft has touched the runway. If they are accidentally put in operation while the plane is still in the air they can cause it to drop like a dead bird.

On the DC-8 of the early 1970's, the spoilers were operated by a two-way lever. It was the co-pilot's job to either *push* the lever just before landing, in which case the flaps would open automatically the moment the wheels touched the runway, or to *pull* the lever at the moment of touchdown, which would open the flaps instantly. Naturally, the co-pilot had to remember to push the spoiler control-lever, not pull it, while the jet was still in the air.

On May 5, 1970, an Air Canada DC-8 was landing at Pearson International Airport in Toronto, then called Malton Airport. The pilot, Pete Hamilton, and the co-pilot were busy in the cockpit. There was much to do while the fully loaded craft made its final approach. When the plane was 15 metres above the runway, the co-pilot reached for the spoiler control-lever. But then, instead of pushing it to engage the automatic mode he made the fatal mistake of pulling it to the manual mode, opening the spoilers too soon.

Immediately the aircraft dropped the 15 metres and flopped onto the runway, the right wing smacking into the ground. The black box recorded the pilot shouting, "No! No! No!" and the co-pilot saying, "Sorry! Oh, sorry, Pete." Hamilton decided to take off and fly around again, not knowing one of the engines had been ripped off and jet fuel was pouring out of the right wing. The jet did gain height and started to circle around. But then, suddenly, there were three mighty explosions, the entire right wing fell away and the jet plummeted into a farmer's field, killing all 109 people aboard.

Part of the wreckage of the DC-8 after the fateful mistake.

In the investigation that followed, it was established that the co-pilot had opened the spoilers while the plane was in the air. People wondered how a co-pilot could make such a mistake. In 1971, an American pilot made the very same mistake while on a training flight. Fortunately he was still able to land the plane safely and nobody was hurt. Then, in 1973, an Icelandic Airlines DC-8 co-pilot again pulled the lever instead of pushing it. This time, although there was no fatal crash, there were passengers who were badly hurt. Finally, it is strongly suspected that the same error was responsible for the crash of a Japan Airlines DC-8 in Moscow in 1972.

After years of such errors, the system for operating the spoilers on DC-8's was changed. But the change was made too late for the ill-fated 109 passengers and crew of Air Canada flight 621. On that hot May afternoon the wreckage looked like a garbage dump. The next time you push a door instead of pulling it, remember the terrible mistake that caused the crash of flight 621.

24
Tragedy in the Cold Atlantic

Some of the best sailors in the world come from Newfoundland. Even so, in one of Canada's worst ocean tragedies in recent years many Newfoundlanders died in the cold waters off their own rocky coast. Why?

In this tragedy the Newfoundlanders weren't sailors, and they weren't working aboard a ship. They were stationed on a floating drilling rig called the *Ocean Ranger*. It was anchored in the Atlantic while the workers aboard drilled into the sea bed searching for oil trapped beneath the Grand Banks. About half of them were Canadians, mostly Newfoundlanders, the other half, Americans. The rig itself was owned by an American company.

The most senior person on the rig wasn't a sea captain, or any kind of sailor at all. He was a tool pusher, an expert drilling-rig engineer whose knowledge lay in drilling, not in seamanship. In the urgent business of drilling for oil not a lot of thought was given to safety, or the possible hazards of being at sea. There were lifeboats, but they were of two different kinds, and nobody was sure if all the men knew how to use them. Lifejackets were supplied, but they were the wrong type. There were no "survival suits," which can save a man's life if he falls into freezing water. In fact, some of the lifeboats hadn't even been installed when disaster struck in 1982.

There were basic problems with the design of the *Ocean Ranger* right from the start. The sea-going heart of a drilling rig is the ballast control room. This is the control centre which keeps the vessel floating evenly and steadily. Instead of being placed high up, as a bridge is placed on a ship, where ice and waves have the least chance of doing any damage, it was positioned half-way up one of the giant legs. This kept it above the calm water, but not above the waves of a severe storm.

On Valentine's Day, 1982, the rig was shaken by the howling winds of a freezing winter storm. Huge waves smashed against the floating platform, causing it to shudder and strain against the 12 anchors holding it in place. Then one particularly big wave came crashing through the window of the ballast control room.

Before the operator on duty could do anything, the electrical system was short-circuited by the water

The *Ocean Ranger* before she sank.

that came pouring in. Under emergency circumstances, the operator is expected to use hand controls, but to do that he needs to know how they work. It seems this operator didn't know. To make matters worse, the intercom system connecting the ballast control room with the rest of the rig was no good. At some point it had broken down and never been repaired. At 1:05 a.m. on Sunday, February 15, the foreman of the *Ocean Ranger* radioed that the rig had a port list (a tilt to the left) that couldn't be corrected. This would be bad enough in calm water. In a storm it was disastrous.

The supply ship for the *Ocean Ranger*, the *Seaforth Highlander*, was immediately sent to the rescue, along with the supply ships serving two other drilling rigs. At 1:30 a.m. the *Ocean Ranger* reported that the men had been ordered to take to the lifeboats. One by one the boats were launched into the towering seas by the inexperienced men, and one by one they crashed into the enormous pillars of the rig and sank, or were flipped over by the first wave they encountered.

Now the lack of survival suits became a life-and-death problem. In the freezing Atlantic, every second counted while the supply ships tried desperately to reach the 84 men and women. By the time the *Seaforth Highlander* got to the scene, less than an hour after being dispatched, only one badly damaged lifeboat was found afloat with living people inside. The ship manoeuvred alongside. The frozen passengers were almost within arm's reach of rescue when the lifeboat slowly rolled over, throwing its occupants, some wearing only pyjamas, into the sea. The *Seaforth Highlander* drifted on, and before it could come around again through the waves, the hapless passengers were all dead.

For hours the three supply ships criss-crossed the area. By about 3:00 a.m. the *Ocean Ranger* itself had sunk completely from sight, leaving the sea littered with wreckage and floating bodies. Not one person aboard the drilling rig survived.

An investigation by the Canadian and Newfoundland governments found flaws in the operation of the rig by its American owners. The disaster was directly linked to equipment failures and poor training. Every drilling rig is now under the overall command of a sea captain who has the last word on safety. Practice emergencies are held regularly, and workers are sometimes fired if they fail to attend. The loss of 84 lives and a multi-million dollar drilling rig taught the oil industry what the sailors of Newfoundland have always known: *The sea must be respected.*

25

The Vancouver Fire

Vancouver is one of Canada's most beautiful cities and a world-class seaport and industrial centre. Like most Canadian cities, it suffered a major fire in its early years.

The fur traders and gold miners were the first to come to the B.C. coast, and when they moved on, the lumber mills moved in. Suddenly sawmills appeared on nearly every river, and towns like Port Moody and New Westminster looked as if they would attract all the new settlers. But then the small town of Granville, nicknamed Gastown, later to be called Vancouver, became the last stop for the newly built CPR railroad. Vancouver grew like a wild thing, spreading out on to nearby hillsides and the tree-lined mountain slopes. Forests were stripped of their timber, and leftover branches and stumps, called slash, lay drying in heaps at the edge of every road and clearing.

Vancouver in 1885 before the fire.

The hot sun in 1886 dried the slash completely and baked the ground to a hard, dusty brown. On June 13, a fire began somewhere in the woods to the north. The busy new town lay directly in its path, and the people, recognizing the deadly situation, began to run. For some, staying long enough to put on a pair of shoes was too long. Many were trapped by the flames. Most ran for the safety of the cool salt water of Burrard Inlet.

According to one witness, the houses would "blister on the bare boards and shimmer a moment or

Vancouver policemen outside the makeshift city hall one day after the fire.

two with the heat waves. Then the whole outside of the building would be a mass of white flame."

In one part of town people huddled in a ditch while those just a few metres away burned to death. Others who hid in wells suffocated when the oxygen in the air was consumed by the fire. Those in Burrard Inlet escaped death by building rafts and pushing them out into the water. It was too dangerous to stay on the shore.

After a few hours, the fire burned itself out. The amazing thing is the speed with which the city was

Vancouver after the fire.

rebuilt. Tents were erected to replace stores and the smouldering city hall. Cities that usually competed with Vancouver helped out. New Westminster sent lumber that very day, along with $9000 in cash — a lot of money in those days. Within 12 hours, the actual rebuilding had begun. Vancouver soon grew bigger than it had been before, and it has been growing ever since.

26
The Victoria Day Disaster

On May 24, 1881, a crowded ferry boat on the Thames River in London, Ontario, collapsed and sank, killing 181 people. It was a terrible loss to the town.

In the 1870's, the Thames River was dammed so there would be pressure for the new fire hydrants throughout London. The council was very aware of the dangers fire represented and wanted to make sure there would be no tragedies in their town. The newly widened river that resulted from the damming was perfect for ferryboats and ferryboat rides. A child could take a long ride down the river and back for 10¢. Adults had to pay a whopping 15¢. The ferry passed Springbank Park, Woodland Cemetery and Sulphur Springs Health Spa. As it cruised slowly by each dock, people would jump on or off. Sometimes the more adventurous jumped from ferry to ferry as they passed each other on the river. Safety laws were more lax then than they are now.

In the late 1800's, people worked hard six days a week. And the seventh day, Sunday, was strictly observed as a day of rest. Games and picnics weren't considered to be "rest," so public holidays like Victoria Day were eagerly awaited as days to be really enjoyed. A ferryboat captain by the name of Rankin had a particular affection for Victoria Day. His ferry was named the *Victoria*. But Victoria Day, 1881, turned out to be the worst day of his life.

The day began well enough. But then, in the afternoon, another ferry, the *Forest City*, ran aground on a sandbar. This meant the *Victoria* had to carry extra passengers back from Springbank Park. By the time the Victoria arrived, the tired and hot crowd had been waiting a long time. Hundreds clambered aboard. Captain Rankin was concerned about the numbers crowding onto his ferry and warned of the dangers of overcrowding, but only a few people got off. The ferry moved on up the river and the passengers, happy now to be on their way home, cheered and waved as they passed other boats. But as the *Victoria* steamed slowly along, it began to sink lower and lower in the water. Soon the lower deck was awash. The craft had a small leak in her underside and was slowly sinking. When he realized this, Captain Rankin decided to beach her.

Just as he was steering toward the nearest sandbank, the passengers, not knowing the danger

The *Victoria*.

they were in, crowded onto one side of the ferry to watch a canoe race. The vessel responded with a dangerous list. The sudden lurch tipped the big steam boiler free and it careered across the deck, scalding passengers and knocking them into the water. The boiler knocked away pillars that supported the crowded upper deck and it too came crashing down. And then, as all this was happening, the ferry rolled right over. Hundreds of passengers were trapped and there was tremendous panic as people fought for their lives in the muddy water, clawing and climbing over each other to get to the surface. Some came up gasping for air, only to be pulled under again by those coming up from below them.

John Carling, owner of Carling Breweries, was riding by in his horsedrawn cart at the time. He and his driver, Frank Moore, rescued many people. Mose Cox of Westminster saved 30 people unaided, and helped to rescue 35 more. Despite these efforts, 181 people died. A man named Thomas Stevens lost his whole family and had to be restrained from jumping into the river to drown himself in his grief.

Later, an inquest ruled that ferries should be made stronger if they were to carry passengers on the Thames. The tragedy was so terrible, however, that no ferries ventured onto the river for another 10 years.

27
A Week of Fear

Near midnight on Saturday, November 10, 1979, a freight train rolled steadily through quiet Mississauga, Ontario. It was over a kilometre long and carried explosive gases like propane, burnable liquids like tuolene, and a deadly gas, chlorine. Slowly it rumbled past houses where people slept.

It passed factories and highrise apartment buildings, and people slept on. But dogs and cats awoke and listened to sounds human ears couldn't detect. There was something very wrong with the train: an axle on one of the cars wasn't getting any oil. It had become what railway men call a "hot box." With no oil to cool it, it got so hot that it began to glow, squealing protest in pitches too high for anyone to detect.

Finally the friction and heat became too great, and the wheels and axle broke away from the tuolene car they were under and rolled into a quiet backyard.

The tank car dragged on down the track, pushed along by the many heavy cars behind it. In places the dragging car snapped the sturdy railroad ties like toothpicks. Flames danced in the darkness, but because of the many bends and curves in the track the engineer and brakeman at the front of the train couldn't see what was going on.

Then, at Mavis Road crossing, the tank car slipped sideways and finally came off the track. The cars behind piled into it, and in seconds there was a giant zigzag of tank cars lying crumpled together on the tracks. The engineer knew there was a problem only when the automatic brakes locked on the front cars and dragged the powerful diesel engines to a halt. Larry Krupa, the brakeman, went back along the line. He was in the process of releasing the brakes when the flames ignited a tank car and turned it into an exploding missile that rocketed through the air, missing him by less than a hundred metres.

The derailment had taken place in one of the very few places in Mississauga where there is an open space around the railway tracks, the first of many miracles to be seen that long week in November. Had the car derailed a minute earlier or later, it would have been beside apartment buildings or houses, and the exploding cars would have killed many people. The ball of flame from the exploding tank car was seen for several kilometres, and people in nearby

The emergency over, a fireman inspects the ruptured chlorine tank.

Toronto and Oakville heard and felt the explosion.

Firefighters rushed to the scene and set up hoses to spray the wrecked tank cars. But the cars kept exploding and shooting through the air, and the firefighters were constantly sprinting for cover. By another miracle, none of the cars landed near firefighters or emergency workers on the scene.

It soon became known that one of the tank cars contained chlorine gas. Chlorine is used today in swimming pools and household products, but in World War I the gas was used to kill soldiers. Its yellowish-green cloud would stay near the ground and choke the soldiers as they hid in their trenches.

There was enough chlorine in the tank car to kill a whole army—or a whole city.

The heads of the police and fire departments, the Mississauga mayor and many other emergency workers were on the scene quickly. Mississauga officials had a plan for coping with emergencies, and now they put it into effect. Police Chief Burroughs ordered a large part of Mississauga to be evacuated. If the chlorine car ruptured, the gas would kill anyone near, including any deep sleepers who might still be in bed. Within an hour the area was deserted. People stayed with friends and relatives or in emergency shelters that were quickly set up in schools and shopping malls.

At the scene of the accident, firefighters sweated in the heat while small amounts of leaking chlorine gas and other chemicals made their eyes smart and water. They used hoses to cool off the fire and hoped much of the propane and other flammable chemicals would burn off. The wind direction changed, and with the change came a new order to evacuate. Another section of Mississauga was cleared of people, and the emergency shelters were suddenly even more crowded. Experts in handling chlorine spills were rushed to the scene, but they were unable to suggest a way to patch the leaking tank car. All attempts to plug the hole failed.

Bulldozers begin the massive job of cleaning up after the derailment.

Meanwhile the danger increased to the point where yet another section of Mississauga was evacuated. In all, nearly a quarter of a million people had to leave their homes during the emergency. Some were unable to return for six days. Volunteer workers and police patrolled the streets and kept unauthorized people out. Residents of the suburban city were worried about pets and plants they hadn't brought with them, so policemen and volunteers went into houses to feed the hungry animals.

Eventually a way was found to use heavy duty air bags to plug the hole in the leaking tank car. The dangerous chlorine gas was mixed with caustic soda to make it harmless, and the people of Mississauga were allowed to return to their homes. So ended the biggest evacuation in North America, all without a single loss of life: another miracle.

Trains like the one that derailed in Mississauga pass through Canadian towns and cities every day. Each year about 300 trains derail in Canada, but most of them go off the track in lonely, faraway places. Even so, government studies are recommending that trains carrying dangerous chemicals be watched carefully and that cars containing chlorine and other poisons be painted bright colours so they can be easily seen if there is a wreck.

28

The Wreck of the *Princess Sophia*

On a lonely reef off the coast of Alaska lie the remains of a Canadian passenger ship, the *Princess Sophia*. Within sight of land, and just a few kilometres from rescue ships, the liner was torn open on the sharp reef, where she then sank with the loss of all aboard.

On the morning of October 24, 1918, the *Princess Sophia* was caught in a blizzard and driven off course. Running at full speed, the ship crashed onto the rocks of Vanderbilt Reef and lodged there. Captain Locke was confident that although his vessel was stuck right then, the next high tide would lift it clear. There were no holes in the hull. Details of the situation were radioed to the owners of the ship, Canadian Pacific Railway in Victoria, assuring them that everyone on board was safe.

The CPR decided to take no chances and sent another ship, the *Princess Alice*, to bring the passengers back, as well as a salvage ship to help the

The *Princess Sophia* at sea.

Princess Sophia. American ships also heard the radio exchanges and they too steamed to the aid of the *Princess Sophia*. They hove to, ready to take those aboard to the nearby shore. But Captain Locke decided there was no need to disturb the passengers unduly by having them spend an uncomfortable night, especially with the snow falling heavily. After all, the sea was flat and calm and they were warm and safe on board the ship, and that was where they wanted to stay.

But then, with no warning, the falling snow turned into a wicked storm. The wind rose to a howl and huge waves, metres high, sprang out of the flat sea to pummel the small American rescue ships

The *Princess Sophia* on Vanderbilt Reef.

anchored around the *Sophia*. They retreated quickly to the shelter of a small island nearby. Now the wind began to move the *Princess Sophia* as well. A particularly strong gust pushed the stern of the ship around, and the bottom of the hull tore on the rocks like tinfoil. The shift also dislodged the ship. She drifted free and immediately began to sink. The radio operator signalled, "Just in time to say goodbye. We are foundering." In the howling storm the small American ships were unable to get through to the dying vessel, so close by. The other CPR ships were still a long way off.

By the morning of the 25th, only the short mast at the bow of the *Princess Sophia* could be seen above the water. Bodies floated everywhere. It was the sad duty of the captain of the *Princess Alice* to report that not one person from the ship had survived the night. All 343 men, women and children were dead. Before they perished, two men did manage to swim to the shore about six kilometres away. One was found in a sitting position on the beach, frozen. The other was found at the end of a short trail of meandering footsteps, face down in the sand.

One sea captain later claimed that the water was so calm before the storm that the passengers could have been safely taken ashore by canoe. The sinking of this proud Canadian Pacific ship remains the worst disaster at sea on our west coast.

Further Reading

If you would like to know more, here is a list of other books about Canada and Canadian disasters:

Anvil of the Gods, by Fred McClement. Published by J.B. Lippincott Company, 1964.

B.C. Disasters, by Derek Pethick. Published by Stagecoach Publications, Langley, B.C, 1978.

The Beothuks or Red Indians, by James P. Hawley. Published by Coles Publishing Co. Ltd., 1980.

Darkest Hours, by Jay Robert Nash. Published by Nelson Hall, 1976.

Death on the Ice, by Cassie Brown. Published by Doubleday Canada Ltd., 1974.

The Developing Human, by K.L. Moore. Published by W.B. Saunders and Co., 1977.

Dying Hard: The Ravages of Industrial Disease, by Elliot Leyton. Published by McClelland and Stewart, 1975.

Extinction: The Beothuks of Newfoundland, by Frederick W. Rowe. Published by McGraw-Hill Ryerson, 1977.

Fourteen Minutes, by James Croall. Published by Michael Joseph Ltd., London, England, 1978.

Great Canadian Disasters, by Frank Rasky. Published by Longman Canada Ltd., 1961.

Great Lakes Shipwrecks and Survivals, by William Ratigan. Published by Wm. B. Ferdmans Pub. Co., Grand Rapids, 1960.

Hot Box, by Jack Cahill. Published by Paperjacks, 1980.

Hurricane Hazel, by Betty Kennedy. Published by Macmillan Co. of Canada, 1979.

It Doesn't Matter Where You Sit, by Fred McClement. Published by McClelland and Stewart, 1966.

Lake Huron, by Fred Landon. Published by Bobbs Merrill Co., New York, 1949.

Miracle Town: Springhill, Nova Scotia, by James B. Brown. Published by Lancelot Press, Hartsport, N.S., 1983.

Murder for Fun, The Rape and Slaughter of the Beothuk Indians of Newfoundland, by Ernest Kelly. Published by Highway Book Shop Publishers, Cobalt, Ontario, 1974.

My Country, by Pierre Berton. Published by McClelland and Stewart, 1976.

Regina, the Queen City, by Earl G. Drake. Published by McClelland and Stewart, 1955.

Shananditti: The Last of the Beothuks, by Keith Winter. Published by J.J. Douglas Ltd., B.C., 1975.

Shipwreck, Piracy and Terror in the Northwest, by T.W. Patterson. Published by Solitaire Publications, 1972.

Suffer the Children: The Story of Thalidomide, by the *Sunday Times* Insight Team. Published by Viking Press, New York, 1979.

True Tales of the Great Lakes, by Dwight Boyer. Published by Dodd Mead and Co., New York, 1971.

Shipwrecks of British Columbia, by Fred Rogers. Published by J.J. Douglas Ltd., Vancouver, 1983.

The Vancouver Book, Edited by Chuck Davis. Published by Evergreen Press Ltd., Vancouver, 1976.

Victoria Day Disaster, by Kenneth D. McTaggart. Published by Skinner Printing Co., Petrolia, Ontario, 1978.

Photo Credits